Virtual Tax

Virtual Tax: The taxation of virtual currency

Published by Desert Mystery Publishing

ISBN: 0-9842205-2-6
ISBN-13: 978-0-9842205-2-6

www.tucsontaxteam.com
info@tucsontaxteam.com
(520) 777-7844

Cover credit: Mariah Wall
Editor-in-chief: Gary Payne

Virtual Tax:
The taxation of virtual currency

by Amy M. Wall, EA, MBA

For Mona Coury, the Tax Goddess

Important Notice:

This book is designed to provide information on the taxation of virtual currency to the best of the author's understanding as of the date of publication. Tax law as it pertains to virtual currency is very much in its infancy; future guidance is very much needed to clarify many issues. The author and publisher do not guarantee or warrant any information contained herein; competent professional advice should always be sought for your particular situation.

Further, the author and publisher are not engaged in legal services and no information contained herein should be construed as legal advice.

Table of Contents

Preface

IF YOU'RE READING THIS BOOK, I assume you have some familiarity with virtual currency: Bitcoin, Ethereum, Litecoin, Dogecoin, PotCoin, Peercoin, whatever. My purpose here is not to rehash the history, virtues, or pitfalls of virtual currency, but to discuss the tax implications of earning, paying, investing, selling, giving, or inheriting virtual currency.

From a tax standpoint, the difficulty presented by virtual currency is simply this: it's often used as a currency but taxed as property. Because it is taxed as property, there are taxable gains and losses upon sale. Because it is also used as currency, purchases and sales occur frequently and often in micro amounts.

Lest we wrongfully lay blame at the IRS' door, it's worth noting that the IRS really had no choice but to classify virtual currency as property. The legal tender of the United States is the dollar; anything that varies in value when measured against that legal tender has the possibility of generating income. And income is, well . . . taxable.

Virtual currency was officially pronounced to be property when the IRS published Notice 2014-21. This Notice caused much hand-wringing because it puts a huge record-keeping burden on users of virtual currency.

Based on the emails and phone calls I receive, I've concluded that most virtual currency users are in a bit of a fog concerning the tax implications of Notice 2014-21. This booklet is intended to help dispel some of that fog.

Disclaimer: *This booklet is intended as a general commentary on virtual currency taxation. It is not intended to represent tax law, nor is it intended to apply to any reader's particular tax situation. It is no substitute for the advice of your own tax professional. As an IRS Circular 230 practitioner, I have no responsibility for any positions you take on your tax return, unless I have prepared and signed that tax return. For detailed analysis of your tax situation, please consult your tax advisor.*

Remember that the tax law which applies to virtual currency is in its early stages, and future alterations are likely. As with virtual currency in general, you proceed at your own risk. The author owns some virtual currency, but has no vested interest in any particular platform or corporation.

Part I:
The Basics of Virtual Currency Taxation

1
Notice 2014-21

ON MARCH 15, 2014, THE IRS officially declared virtual currency to be property via Notice 2014-21. A Notice is usually issued prior to being officially published in the Internal Revenue Bulletin; the Bulletin is the ultimate authority and the Notice is simply a preview of what's going into the IRB. So yes, the Notice is official IRS guidance.

I suggest you read the Notice, included in the back of this book as Appendix 1, in its entirety. For those who can't get past the tax-speak of the Notice, here's a quick and dirty summation: **Virtual currency is property. Payment received as virtual currency must be included as taxable income; to determine the amount of income to include, convert the virtual currency received to dollars using the fair market value of that virtual currency on the date of receipt. The character of gain or loss depends on the character of the virtual currency in the hands of the taxpayer. Mining of virtual currency creates income for the miner—again, at the fair market value of the currency on** the date of receipt. Further, mining constitutes a trade or business and is thus subject to self-employment tax; virtual currency received by an independent contractor in exchange for goods and services is also subject to self-employment tax. The reporting and back-up withholding required of an employer or other payee paying in US dollars is also required of an employer or other payee paying in virtual currency. Taxpayers who did not comply with the requirements of this notice prior to its date of issue may be subject to penalties.

The rest of this book will discuss the details of the Notice and the implications that arise; it will also provide suggestions as to how to comply with the intent of the IRS.

2
Earning Virtual Currency

IF YOU ARE EARNING VIRTUAL currency in exchange for services, you are earning money. You must pay tax on the dollar value of that money at the time of "constructive receipt". The issue of constructive receipt is an important one in Tax World. Constructive receipt is defined as that moment when the funds are available to the taxpayer without substantial limitations. If a check is available to you but you haven't cashed it, you have nonetheless constructively received it. If you must travel to Japan to get the money and you hadn't expected to have to make the trip at that time, then you might be considered not to have had constructive receipt until you actually made the trip and received the money. (But then you might have to prove that you hadn't expected to make the trip.)

The concept of constructive receipt is going to be an important one in the world of virtual currency as well, because the value of virtual currency can vary substantially. A dollar today is a dollar tomorrow, but a bitcoin today isn't likely to have the same dollar value tomorrow.

Under the doctrine of constructive receipt, you have received income as soon as the virtual currency hits your wallet or becomes available to you in a similar way. Generally, the exchange you are using will give you the dollar value of that income upon receipt. If you don't have an exchange helping you out, then it becomes entirely your responsibility to determine the value of the received virtual currency, document how you calculated that value, and retain that documentation. It isn't the IRS' job to calculate the income you received; it's your job to calculate and prove the value of that income if asked to do so.

Remember that you are required to pay tax on any income you receive, whether or not you spend it. Even if you leave that virtual currency in your wallet for the next ten years, it's still considered taxable income upon receipt. When you do spend the virtual currency there's another taxable event—but let's not get too far ahead.

Since virtual currency isn't generally used to pay employees, most people who earn virtual currency are treated as self-employed. These taxpayers file a Schedule C with their 1040 returns and bear the responsibility for paying their own Social Security and Medicare taxes as well as income taxes. If you aren't sure whether or not you are self-employed, the bottom line is this: if the person paying you virtual currency doesn't withhold Social Security and

Medicare taxes for you (and does not generate a tax form at the end of the year to tell you how much they withheld) then paying these taxes is up to you. Employees get help in paying these taxes: their employer withholds 6.2% of their wages for Social security and 1.45% for Medicare and then matches that amount, sending in a total of 12.4% for Social Security and 2.90% for Medicare. If you don't have an employer to help you, then you've got to pay that 15.3% tax all by yourself. When you add income tax to that 15.3%, you can owe quite a bit to the IRS when you file your return.

In addition, if you owe a substantial amount to the IRS and don't meet the requirements for exceptions, you will also have to pay an underpayment penalty and interest on the unpaid tax and penalty. To avoid penalties and interest, you should make quarterly tax payments throughout the year or increase your federal withholding on income from other sources.

Of course, being self-employed means you can deduct ordinary and necessary business expenses from your income. If you work from your home, it's possible that you can deduct part of your home expenses as an office-in-home. If your work requires you to purchase equipment or software, you may be able to deduct those expenses. Always retain documentation supporting those expenses.

So, if you are earning virtual currency, be proactive: talk to your tax preparer about estimating your income and expenses so that you can make adequate estimated tax payments. If you get a blank stare when you ask about estimating income and expenses, find a better tax preparer.

If you function as a retail store or online business and you accept virtual currency as payment for the goods and services you provide, then you're responsible for translating that virtual currency into its dollar value and reporting it as income.

You are required by law to report income even if you have not received documentation such as a 1099-MISC or a W-2 from the person who hired you, and even if you receive it in cash. (I'm not commenting on the likelihood of you getting caught if you don't report it; I'm stating the law of Tax World.)

Final note: if you don't immediately convert your earned virtual currency into dollars, another reportable transaction awaits you: sale or loss upon sale of virtual currency. See Chapter 5 for details.

3
Paying with Virtual Currency

NOTICE 2014-21 SPECIFICALLY STATES THAT payment made using virtual currency is subject to information reporting. If, in the course of your trade or business, you pay an individual (not a corporation) virtual currency worth $600 or more in a calendar year, you are required to issue that individual Form 1099-MISC and send a copy to the IRS. As with everything else in Tax World, the forms are set up to report in dollars; this means that you'll have to determine the dollar value of the virtual currency you paid out as of the date you paid it. And—you guessed it—you must also retain documentation showing how you calculated that amount.

If you are paying interest in virtual currency, then plan on issuing the payee a 1099-INT; again, it's up to you to determine and document the dollar value of the virtual currency that you paid.

Notice 2014-21 specifically states that payment of virtual currency is subject to what's called "backup withholding". If you are going to pay someone virtual currency worth $600 or more in a calendar year and that person has refused to give you a tax ID number (social security number or EIN), you are required to withhold 28% of that income and send it to the IRS. (You'll have to send it in dollars; the IRS does not yet accept virtual currency.) Failure to send in backup withholding if you are required to do so can be penalized at a rate of $500 for a civil penalty, and $1,000 and/or imprisonment for a criminal penalty.

Again, be proactive. If you plan to pay someone $600 or more in the course of your trade or business, have that person fill out a Form W-9 before you even begin. Pay no attention to the inevitable whining, and don't let them start work—no matter how eager you both are—until that form is completely filled out and signed.

If you are an employer who pays employees in virtual currency, you are responsible for meeting the same payroll reporting requirements as any other employer—you just have to remember to convert the payments of virtual currency into dollars. An employer's failure to file and pay payroll taxes is heavily penalized. These penalties can be levied on the business, the business owner, and any other "responsible parties". I strongly advise you to take payroll reporting and withholding requirements quite seriously.

The IRS requires employers to retain payroll records for a minimum of three years. However, when records are connected to property, the IRS states that records should be kept until the period of limitations expires for the year in which the property is disposed of. It isn't yet clear what this latter requirement means for employers who pay in virtual currency, aka property.

Reporting requirements are far easier for 1099 workers than for employees, but be aware that the distinction between an employee and an independent contractor is a matter of facts and circumstances, not a matter of opinion or preference. There are stiff penalties for treating someone as an independent contractor when they are actually an employee, so it's important to know the difference. The distinction between employee and independent contractor is based on three factors: Behavioral, Financial and Type of Relationship. Read IRS guidance to determine the reality of your own situation.

Finally, let's not forget that paying your household employee in virtual currency is no different than paying that person with dollars. A household employee can be a housekeeper, maid, nanny, gardener, etc. If you pay any one of these workers $2,000 or more (as of 2017) then you are generally required to withhold Social Security and Medicare tax. Typically, the painter, plumber and handyman are independent contractors, and so you are not responsible for paying their Social Security and Medicare taxes for them.

Failure to file any of the required forms can lead to penalties under IRC §6721, *Failure to file correct information returns* and §6722, *Failure to furnish correct payee statements.*

4
Investing in Virtual Currency

BECAUSE VIRTUAL CURRENCY IS CONSIDERED property, gains and losses that arise from investing in virtual currency must be reported as short-term or long-term gains or losses. The good news is that if you hold virtual currency for one year or more, gains are treated as capital gains and taxed at a favorable rate. That favorable rate can save you thousands of tax dollars. As of this writing, taxpayers in the 10% and 15% brackets pay no tax on long-term gains. Taxpayers in the top 39.6% bracket pay 20% on capital gains. And everyone in the brackets between pays 15% on capital gains.

Short-term gains are taxed at ordinary income rates. Capital losses can be used to offset capital gains; but, as with stocks or other property, the amount of loss that can be used to offset *ordinary* income is limited to $3,000 per year; the rest is rolled forward and used against future gains. This $3,000 limit was put in place in 1978, and has never been raised. If it had been adjusted for inflation, that $3,000 would be $12,000 today. Complain to your Congressperson.

Gain or loss is calculated by subtracting your cost basis from your proceeds. To put it as simply as possible, let's say that in April of 2015, you purchased ten BTC for $236 each, for a total of $2,360. In May of 2016, you decided to sell these ten BTC for $531 each, or $5,310. You have a long-term capital gain of $2,950.

> Sale price: $5,310
> Cost basis: ($2,360)
> Gain: $2,950

Now let's add one small wrinkle: transaction fees. You paid fees when you purchased the BTC, so add these fees to the purchase price. If you paid $46 in fees, your cost basis would be $2,360 + $46 = $2406. You paid fees when you sold the BTC. If your fees were $79, your proceeds would be $5,310 - $79 = $5,231. So your gain would be $5,231 - $2,406 = $2,825. Because you held these BTC for more than one year, you would pay tax at the preferred capital gain rate, rather than at the ordinary income rate.

In this example, you knew your cost basis because either a) you kept a record of it, b) you use a wallet that kept a record of it or c) you looked it up online. That's easy enough. Now, let's say you sell those BTC in May of 2016, but have no idea what you paid for it or when you got it. Without proof of basis, the IRS can choose to assume a worst-case scenario: a basis of zero and a purchase date of less than a year of the sale date. With these worst-case assumptions, you'd pay tax on the entire gain at ordinary income rates.

Now consider another example: in April of 2015, you bought five BTC for $236 each, for a total of $2,360, and another five BTC in January of 2016 for $365 each, for a total of $1,825. In May of 2016, you sold seven BTC for $531 each. How would you calculate your gain?

You have some leeway here. Notice 2014-21 does not specify which technique you should use to determine which virtual currency you sold. The general consensus seems to be that you have the option to use any of the methods employed by sales of investments: first-in-first-out (FIFO), last-in-first-out (LIFO), specific lot, or average cost. For now, let's keep it simple and use the FIFO method, which is the method the IRS requires you to use for sales of investments if you don't have adequate records for assigning specific prices to each portion of an investment position. We'll discuss other methods in Part II, Chapter 5.

Using the FIFO method, we first sell the BTC that we first purchased back in April of 2015. Let's ignore fees for the moment, just to keep the math easy. As in the first example, we have a long-term capital gain of $2,950. Again, it's considered long-term because you owned those BTC for a year before selling them.

But we still have two more BTC to sell, the ones we purchased in January of 2016 for $365 each, for a total purchase price of $730. We're now selling them for $531 each, for a total sale price of $1,062.

> Sale price: $1,062
> Cost basis: ($730)
> Gain: $332

Because you held these BTC for less than a year, the $332 of gain will be taxed as a short-term capital gain, aka ordinary income.

Incidentally, in Tax World, your holding period actually starts the day *after* you purchased the asset and ends on the day you sell it. If you purchased BTC on April 1st 2015 and sold those same BTC on April 1st 2016, that would be short-term gain. If you sold it on April 2nd of 2016, it would be long-term gain. Pay close attention to your holding period.

Now for a tougher example. I've limiting the number of digits in the number of BTC purchased and sold in order to make this easier to follow: I'm more interested in having you understand the logic behind this process than nit-picking the exact dollar amounts.

Assume you have made the following purchases:

Date	BTC	Total Price
Aug. 15, 2015	1.0670	$282.96
Sept. 15, 2015	0.0723	$16.62
Oct. 15, 2015	2.3642	$602.42

And then you have the following sales:

Date	BTC	Total Price
Aug. 15, 2016	0.1034	$37.10
Oct. 15, 2016	1.0000	$399.48
Nov. 15, 2016	1.2777	$909.67

Your thinking should run like this: OK, I sold 0.1034 BTC on August 15, 2016. What BTC did I sell and what did I pay for it? Using the FIFO method, I sold 0.1034 of the 1.0670 BTC that I purchased back on August 15, 2015. I know I paid $282.96 for 1.067 BTC, so how much did the 0.1034 BTC cost? If you divide $282.96 by 1.067, you quickly discover that the per unit BTC price you paid was $265.19 per BTC. Multiplying that by 0.1034 tells you that 0.1034 BTC cost you $27.42. You sold it for $37.10, so you have a gain of $9.68. Since you didn't wait that extra day, this is a short-term gain.

The next step in your thinking should be this: I sold 1.000 BTC on October 15, 2016. What BTC did I sell and what did I pay for it? Using the FIFO method, I have 1.0670 − 0.1034 = 0.9636 BTC left from that August 15, 2015 purchase. I already know that the per unit price for the BTC I purchased on August 15, 2015 was $265.19. Multiplying that times the 0.9636 BTC gives me $255.54. (Note that you get the same result if you take the full purchase price of $282.96 and subtract the $27.42 that you sold in August 2016.) So I sold 0.9636 BTC worth $255.54; the remaining 1.0000 − 0.9636 =

0.0364 BTC that I sold on October 15, 2016 came from the BTC that I purchased on September 15, 2015. How much did that 0.0364 BTC cost me? The unit price of that BTC was $399.48, so the purchase price of the 0.0364 is $399.48 x 0.0364 = $14.54. Total cost basis of the 1.0000 BTC sold is $255.54 + $14.54 = $270.08. Gain is purchase price minus cost basis: $399.48 - $270.08 = $129.40. And, happily, it's all long-term gain.

Next: I sold 1.2777 BTC on November 15, 2016. What BTC did I sell and what did I pay for them? Well, I've exhausted the batch purchased on August 15, 2015 and I sold 0.0364 of the batch purchased on September 15, 2015, but I've still got 0.0723 − 0.0364 = 0.0359 BTC from that batch. So first I need to sell that. With a unit price of $399.48, the purchase price of 0.0359 was $399.48 x 0.03590 = $14.34. That accounts for 0.0359 of the BTC sold; I still have to account for the remaining 1.2777 − 0.0359 = 1.2416 BTC sold. That all came from the batch I purchased on October 15, 2015. Again, I calculate the unit price of the October batch by dividing $602.42 by 2.3642 = $254.81. I multiply the $254.81 by 1.2416 to get $316.37. Total cost basis of the BTC sold on November 15, 2016 is $14.34 + $316.37 = $330.71. Since the sales proceeds were $909.67, our gain is $909.67 - $330.71 = $578.96. Again, all long-term gain.

This will work if you can keep your wits about you when you work with spreadsheets. If you're really good, you can have fun creating formulas and making it work for you. But if the entire above discussion made you feel like you want to pass out, then you need to get some help with this as soon as possible. Either find someone who can maintain your spreadsheets, pay for an account with one of the few virtual currency tax support companies that are starting to spring up, or stick with a platform like Coinbase, which will do at least some of the work for you. Be aware: presenting your tax preparer with hundreds of transactions and asking her to make sense of it is going to either get you laughed out of the office (January through April) or net you a good-sized bill (May through December).

Incidentally, we're already getting questions about setting up an IRA to invest in virtual currency; it isn't yet known if retirement accounts will be permitted to hold such investments.

5
Spending Virtual Currency

NOTICE 2014-21 STATES THAT CAPITAL gains and losses depend on whether a "virtual currency is a capital asset in the hands of a taxpayer." If virtual currency is held for any length of time in an account, the IRS is likely to regard this as an investment account.

Since virtual currency is considered property, this means that every time you spend virtual currency, no matter how small the amount, you have created a taxable transaction. EVERY TIME. As of this writing, the IRS has offered no *de minimis* transaction amount to ease this burden, nor has there been any indication that taxpayers will be allowed to maintain one virtual currency account for use entirely as currency (thereby incurring no taxable transactions) and another account for investing purposes only (thereby incurring taxable transactions).

This is a serious problem for taxpayers who base their entire financial lives on virtual currency. Every time they buy a cup of coffee with that handy bitcoins-to-dollars debit card, they create a taxable transaction. A better strategy from the viewpoint of Tax World would be to periodically convert a larger amount of virtual currency into dollars—perhaps once a week or once a month—thereby limiting the number of transactions you must cope with.

If you are earning virtual currency and don't want to deal with reporting capital gains, the solution is simply to convert your earnings to dollars immediately upon receipt. You'll still have to report the earnings, but you won't have to report a sale every time you convert some virtual currency to dollars.

It's worth stressing that just because the reporting is onerous doesn't mean the IRS won't require it.

6
Fair Market Value

NOTICE 2014-21 SPECIFICALLY STATES THAT taxpayers must report the fair market value of their virtual currency as of the *date* that the currency was received. Not the time, mind you, the date.

We can imagine some interesting situations because, as you know, the value of virtual currency fluctuates in value from minute to minute. As long as the virtual currency has not been converted to actual cash, the fair market value may be subject to interpretation. The taxpayer may choose to use the average price on the day of receipt, or the price as of the moment of receipt, or the day's high, or the day's low. And different taxpayers may choose differently; someone paying a worker with virtual currency may choose to use that day's high, while the person receiving the wages may choose to use the day's low. And one taxpayer may use different methods at different times; who wouldn't be tempted to go with a higher price when purchasing the virtual currency and the lower option when selling it?

At this point in time, we don't know if taxpayers will be required to use a consistent methodology or the methodology of their choosing for each decision point.

Part II:
Advanced Topics

Part II.

Advanced Topics

1
Giving or Donating Virtual Currency

LET'S SAY YOUR FAVORITE CHARITY—ANY approved 501(c) (3) organization approved by the IRS for tax-deductible donations—is short-sighted and only accepts donations in dollars. So you sell some virtual currency in order to make a donation, thereby incurring either a capital gain or a capital loss. You then would be allowed to deduct the full fair market value of that donation, plus fees involved in the sale, up to 50% of your adjusted gross income. If you donate more than 50% of your adjusted gross income, you can roll the unused donation amount forward for up to five years.

But perhaps this wonderful charitable organization has a merchant account that allows them to accept virtual currency. In this case, you could donate actual virtual currency as PROPERTY. This means that if you had held that virtual currency for one year plus one day or longer, you get to deduct the fair market value of that currency as of the date of the donation, without having to cash it in and pay the capital gains tax. If you donate property that has been held for less than one year and one day, you only get to deduct what you paid for it.

When donating property, you are only allowed to deduct up to 30% of your adjusted gross income; again, any remaining deduction rolls forward for up to five years.

Be aware, also, that there are reporting requirements involved in the donation of property. If you give property valued at more than $500, you are required to include Form 8283 with your tax return. If the virtual currency you donated was worth more than $5,000, you are required to get an appraisal of the property (which you must send in with your tax return) and a written and signed acknowledgement from the charity stating the value of the property you donated. There's an exception for this get-an-appraisal requirement for donations of publicly traded stock, since the value of stock is available on the stock exchange. It would be nice if a similar exception would be put into place for virtual currency, but we don't yet have IRS guidance on this.

Note, please, that you can't get around this by donating lots of small amounts; you're expected to group your deductions with other similar items. (You can avoid the hassle, of course, by donating $4,999 worth of virtual currency.)

Remember that charitable donations are itemized deductions; making the donations help you from a tax standpoint only if you itemize deductions. This is true even if you are a small business filing a Schedule C or filing as an S Corporation. Donations do not reduce the taxable income of the business; they flow over to Schedule A as itemized deductions. If the taxpayer doesn't itemize, then there is no tax benefit to the donation. (A discussion of the karmic benefits of the donation is beyond the scope of this book.)

Then there are those donations that are not tax-deductible. When you give virtual currency to a person or organization that is not a 501(c) (3) organization, you have made a gift, not a donation. No worries for you; as long as you don't give any single person/organization more than $14,000, you have no tax obligations whatsoever. The same is not true of the recipient. The person/organization receiving that virtual currency must value it at the fair market value as of the date of receipt, and use that as the cost basis when selling it. This is the principle that will be applied to virtual currency "tips" given online as well.

2
Inheriting Virtual Currency

SINCE VIRTUAL CURRENCY IS PROPERTY, it seems reasonable to apply property inheritance rules to virtual currency. And this is entirely good news.

When someone dies, their property generally passes on to the beneficiaries at the fair market value at the time of death or at an alternate valuation date (exactly six months after death) if the estate executor so chooses. A taxpayer who bought virtual currency when it was inexpensive can pass that currency on to his or her heirs and entirely avoid capital gains tax. But read the fine print: if the heirs are cunning and give their virtual currency to dear old dad less than a year before his death with the idea of getting it back with a fair market value basis, they will be in for a surprise: the IRS wasn't born yesterday. The heirs will get that currency back with an adjusted basis equal to dear old dad's adjusted basis at the time of his death. Further discussion regarding the adjusted basis of gifted assets is beyond the scope of this book: talk to your tax advisor.

If you inherit virtual currency, document its fair market value as of the date of the decedent's death. If you sell it immediately, you must report the sale, but you should incur no taxable gain; you may, in fact, sustain a deductible loss because of the selling fees.

3
Losses of Virtual Currency

IF YOUR VIRTUAL CURRENCY HAS been stolen, lost, or has vanished in a defunct exchange, there may be tax help.

Tax World provides two mechanisms for dealing with these situations. If you have a theft or casualty loss, the loss is reported as an itemized deduction and is calculated as follows: start with the lesser of the property's tax basis (aka what you paid for it plus fees) or the fair market value on the date of the loss. Then subtract $100 per event (per event, not per coin); then deduct 10% of your adjusted gross income. The remaining amount is your deduction.

If you have a capital loss, it's reported on Schedule D. Using this mechanism, your starting point is your original basis (aka what you paid for it plus fees) and the sales price is zero. Thus, you have a loss equivalent to your original investment. If the currency was worth more than what you paid for it at the time of the loss, too bad for you.

It isn't clear, however, that you get to choose which mechanism you prefer. Generally, if you have had money stolen, then you have a theft loss and thus an itemized deduction. If you have a security that becomes worthless, IRC §165 permits you to take a capital loss; this section defines a security as:

(A) a share of stock in a corporation

(B) a right to subscribe for, or to receive, a share of stock in a corporation; or

(C) a bond, debenture, note or certificate, or other evidence of indebtedness, issued by a corporation of by a government or political subdivision thereof, with interest coupons or in registered form.

It's the opinion of this author that, given that virtual currency has been defined as property, all losses due to theft, defunct exchanges and other such disasters should be taken as an itemized deduction.

The fine print: the loss is deductible in the year it's discovered by the taxpayer. The loss is allowed only if there is no reasonable chance of recovery. If the chance of recovery is not yet known, then the deduction must wait until the tax year it which it is known.

4
Wash Sales

A WASH SALE IS A situation in which a taxpayer sells a security to reap a tax loss and then immediately buys it again at that reduced price. For example, you buy Stock ABC when it's $1,000 a share. It drops to $50 a share, but you are ever-hopeful and think it's going to regain its value. You sell it on December 30th at $50 a share, report a tax loss of $1,000 - $50 = $950. Then on January 10th, you sneakily buy Stock ABC back at $50 a share. Nice try; but, again, the IRS wasn't born yesterday. Anytime a security is purchased within 30 days of a "substantially identical" security being sold at a loss, that loss is disallowed.

It's a fair question to wonder if investors in virtual currency will be held to wash sale rules. The IRS Code in question (§1091) specifically refers to shares of stock or securities, so it's hard to see how the rules applying to wash sales would affect virtual currency without the IRS providing some substantive guidance to that effect. At this point, it seems reasonable to suppose that virtual currency traders are exempt from wash sale rules.

Wash Sales

5
Exchanging Virtual Currency

WHEN YOU TRADE ONE VIRTUAL currency for another, you have effectively sold the original virtual currency at its fair market value (thus creating a taxable transaction) and purchased the second virtual currency with the proceeds. The second currency has a cost basis equivalent to the fair market value of the first currency at the time of the trade. Example: let's say you buy one BTC for $265.19 and about six months later, you trade the BTC for some quantity of Ethereum. And let's say that on the day you trade it, the BTC is worth $310.10. You have, effectively, sold that BTC at a gain of $310.10 - $265.19 = $44.91. Your Ethereum has a cost basis of $310.10.

I've been asked frequently if I think the IRS will permit tax-free exchanges, also known as §1031 exchanges, of virtual currency. A §1031 exchange is a series of transactions that allow for the disposal of one asset and the acquisition of a replacement asset without generating a tax liability until the final asset is sold. From IRC §1031:

(a) Nonrecognition of gain or loss from exchanges solely in kind

(1) In general

No gain or loss shall be recognized on the exchange of property held for productive use in a trade or business or for investment if such property is exchanged solely for property of like kind which is to be held either for productive use in a trade or business or for investment.

(2) Exception

This subsection shall not apply to any exchange of—

(A) stock in trade or other property held primarily for sale,

(B) stocks, bonds, or notes,

(C) other securities or evidences of indebtedness or interest,

(D) interests in a partnership,

(E) certificates of trust or beneficial interests, or

(F) choses in action.

(If you're curious about what a chose in action is, it's essentially a right to sue.)

Since the rules government tax-free exchanges include property, and Notice 2014-21 states that virtual currency will be treated as property, there's hope in the virtual currency community that virtual currency held for investment may qualify for §1031 treatment. However, I note that

§1031 specifically states that this exchange will not apply to property held primarily for sale.

Doubtless tax-free exchanges of virtual currency will be tested at some point in a tax court with high-priced attorneys. Unless you'd like to be the guy in that courtroom, I recommend recognizing gain when you exchange virtual currency for other property, even if that other property is another virtual currency.

6
Other Reporting Options

IN PART 1, CHAPTER 4, I stated that while the first-in, first-out (FIFO) method was probably the easiest way to track sales of virtual currency, there are other options. The other options are: last-in, first-out (LIFO), weighted average, and "specific share identification". Which option you choose can have a significant effect on your calculation of gains and losses.

Let's say you have the following BTC purchases:

Lot Date	BTC	Cost Basis	Price Now	Gain (Loss)
Aug. 2015	10	$2,652	$21,800	$19,148
Jan. 2016	10	$3,588	$21,800	$18,212
Aug. 2016	10	$5,672	$21,800	$16,128

Now, suppose that you wanted to sell 10 BTC in July 2017: using the FIFO method, you'd sell the ten BTC you purchased in August of 2015, for a long-term gain of $19,148.

Using the LIFO method, you would sell the BTC

you purchased in August of 2016 for a short-term gain of $16,128.

Using the average-cost method, you'd average out the price: (2,652 + 3,588 + 5,672) ÷ 3 = $3,971 for a gain of $17,829.

Or, using the specific share identification method, you could elect to sell the BTC you purchased in January of 2016 for a long-term gain of $18,212, or any combination of 10 BTC from the three lots. It might seem like a no-brainer to select the LIFO method and pay the lesser capital gains tax, but it might be that you have reasons for paying the higher capital gains this year. Perhaps next year you'll be in a higher tax bracket and thus a higher capital gains tax bracket. Perhaps you plan to sell even more next year, so you want to get as much income moved from next year to this year as possible.

Most virtual currency platforms that track basis specifically utilize LIFO or FIFO to track purchases and sales. If you choose to utilize a different method, you'll have to become quite proficient at spreadsheets, as it could be some time before virtual currency platforms become sophisticated enough to help you out with alternative methods.

From a tax standpoint, the same principles that apply stocks apply to virtual currency: track securities by tax lot if possible; avoid short-term gains; avoid high-turnover in order to minimize fees; harvest losses in order to offset gains. And, of course, buy low and sell high.

7
Foreign Reporting Requirements

NOTICE 2014-21 SPECIFICALLY STATES "UNDER currently applicable law, virtual currency is not treated as currency that could generate foreign currency gain or loss for U.S. federal tax purposes." As of this writing, using or holding virtual currency does not require the filing of an FBAR (Report of Foreign Bank and Financial Accounts). However, it's worth noting that tax law regarding reporting of foreign accounts is not set in concrete.

In June of 2014, in *U.S. vs. John C. Hom*, the federal courts decided that money kept in online poker accounts were, in fact, "...a financial interest in, or signature or other authority over, a bank, securities, or another financial account in a foreign country...." and should have been reported as such. The decision was appealed and was partially overturned and partially upheld. The upshot of all this is that while virtual currency held on a hard drive or printed out on a paper wallet is unlikely to ever fall under FBAR requirements, it is possible that a foreign virtual currency exchange will, sometime in the future, qualify as a foreign financial account. Stay tuned.

8
Preparing Your Tax Return

THE IRS REQUIRES THAT ALL income, including virtual currency income and gains upon sale, be reported on the tax return for the year the income was received. The IRS further expects that documentation supporting the numbers on the tax return will be available for review. To help make sure that all your income is reported, third-party settlement organizations (aka credit card companies) are required to report to the IRS, using Form 1099K, income for any recipient whose number of transactions exceed 200 and total more than $20,000. Coinbase has already stated their intention of complying with this requirement. So if you're receiving significant payments in virtual currency (or any currency, for that matter) through a credit card provider, you can expect the IRS to know all about it.

Failure to properly report income can lead to accuracy related penalties under 26 U.S. Code §6662 – *Imposition of accuracy-related penalty on underpayments*.

If the IRS decides that you've willfully engaged in tax

fraud, it could decide that your case is better handled by the Criminal Investigation branch of the Service. It is not impossible for a careless virtual currency user to face felony tax evasion charges and a federal prison sentence.

9
Audits

IT'S TRUE THAT IT'S BEEN almost pathetically easy to get away with not paying taxes if you use virtual currency. And this fact isn't lost on the IRS. The Service is starting to get very interested in taxpayers who earn/utilize/spend/invest in virtual currency, as was evidenced by recent actions against Coinbase. It is just a matter of time until the legal tangles are untangled and the IRS gets its hands on a whole lot of data that will affect a whole lot of people. When that happens, that whole lot of people are going to be doing a whole lot of scrambling to amend tax returns. My advice is to accept the inevitable and start reporting your income immediately. If you don't understand how to do this yourself, get help. "I didn't understand" is not, has never been, and will never be something the IRS is interested in hearing.

If you believe you could be seriously impacted by an IRS audit, it is far better for you to come forward and amend that tax return sooner rather than later in order to limit penalties and interest. Remember that under normal circumstances, the IRS has only three years to audit you; but there are special cases that can extend that time period. If you omitted more than 25% of your income, that three years becomes six. And if you have committed tax fraud, there is no time limit. Read that again: NO TIME LIMIT. You'll be hiding under the bed for the rest of your life.

Don't count on the much-vaunted anonymity of virtual currency. While it may be possible for some very savvy trader to remain anonymous, this isn't an option for the average user of virtual currency. Your identity is tied to your account by virtue of email contact. And once the IRS can identify a virtual currency account as belonging to an individual, they can extract every transaction from the blockchain.

Furthermore, the IRS does indeed have the resources to engage in the sort of complex data analysis that would be required to track down the owners of the accounts and unravel the blockchain. They'll be aided by tax whistleblowers who receive compensation for providing information that helps the IRS track down virtual currency accounts and owners. And, just as credit card companies are required to report payment transactions made by credit cards by the issuance of a 1099K, it won't be long before virtual currency exchanges will eventually be required to report sales of virtual currency on an as yet undeveloped 1099 form.

Be aware that if your past virtual currency dealings create the potential for criminal charges, you need to speak with a tax attorney, not an Enrolled Agent or CPA.

Only an actual attorney enjoys attorney-client privilege. Unless hired by a tax attorney under a Kovel agreement, an Enrolled Agent or CPA can be subpoenaed by the IRS and become a witness against you.

Disclaimer

I said it before, but for those who weren't listening: *This booklet is intended as a general commentary on virtual currency taxation. It is not intended to represent tax law, nor is it intended to apply to any reader's particular tax situation. It is no substitute for the advice of your own tax professional. As an IRS Circular 230 practitioner, I have no responsibility for any positions you take on your tax return, unless I have prepared and signed that tax return. For detailed analysis of your tax situation, please consult your tax advisor.*

Remember that the tax law which applies to virtual currency is in its early stages, and future alterations are likely. As with virtual currency in general, you proceed at your own risk. The author owns some virtual currency, but has no vested interest in any particular platform or corporation.

Appendix I:
Notice 2014-21

Section 1. Purpose

This notice describes how existing general tax principles apply to transactions using virtual currency. The notice provides this guidance in the form of answers to frequently asked questions.

Section 2. Background

The Internal Revenue Service (IRS) is aware that "virtual currency" may be used to pay for goods or services, or held for investment. Virtual currency is a digital representation of value that functions as a medium of exchange, a unit of account, and/or a store of value. In some environments, it operates like "real" currency—i.e., the coin and paper money of the United States or of any other country that is designated as legal tender, circulates, and is customarily used and accepted as a medium of exchange in the country of issuance—but it does not have legal tender status in any jurisdiction.

Virtual currency that has an equivalent value in real currency, or that acts as a substitute for real currency, is referred to as "convertible" virtual currency. Bitcoin is one example of a convertible virtual currency. Bitcoin can be digitally traded between users and can be purchased for, or exchanged into, U.S. dollars, Euros, and other real or virtual currencies. For a more comprehensive description of convertible virtual currencies to date, see Financial Crimes Enforcement Network (FinCEN) *Guidance on the Application of FinCEN's Regulations to Persons Administering, Exchanging, or Using Virtual Currencies* (FIN-2013-G001, March 18, 2013).

Section 3. Scope

In general, the sale or exchange of convertible virtual currency, or the use of convertible virtual currency to pay for goods or services in a real-world economy transaction, has tax consequences that may result in a tax liability. This notice addresses only the U.S. federal tax consequences of transactions in, or transactions that use, convertible virtual currency, and the term "virtual currency" as used in Section 4 refers only to convertible virtual currency.

No inference should be drawn with respect to virtual currencies not described in this notice. The Treasury Department and the IRS recognize that there may be other questions regarding the tax consequences of virtual currency not addressed in this notice that warrant consideration. Therefore, the Treasury Department and the IRS request comments from the public regarding other types or aspects of virtual currency transactions that should be addressed in future guidance.

Comments should be addressed to:

Internal Revenue Service
Attn: CC:PA:LPD:PR (Notice 2014-21)
Room 5203
P.O. Box 7604
Ben Franklin Station
Washington, D.C. 20044

or hand delivered Monday through Friday between the hours of 8 A.M. and 4 P.M. to:

Courier's Desk
Internal Revenue Service
Attn: CC:PA:LPD:PR (Notice 2014-21)
1111 Constitution Avenue, N.W.
Washington, D.C. 20224

Alternatively, taxpayers may submit comments electronically via e-mail to the following address: Notice.Comments@irscounsel.treas.gov. Taxpayers should include "Notice 2014-21" in the subject line. All comments submitted by the public will be available for public inspection and copying in their entirety.

For purposes of the FAQs in this notice, the taxpayer's functional currency is assumed to be the U.S. dollar, the taxpayer is assumed to use the cash receipts and disbursements method of accounting and the taxpayer is assumed not to be under common control with any other party to a transaction.

Section 4. Frequently Asked Questions

Q-1: How is virtual currency treated for federal tax purposes?

A-1: For federal tax purposes, virtual currency is treated as property. General tax principles applicable to property transactions apply to transactions using virtual currency.

Q-2: Is virtual currency treated as currency for purposes of determining whether a transaction results in foreign currency gain or loss under U.S. federal tax laws?

A-2: No. Under currently applicable law, virtual currency is not treated as currency that could generate foreign currency gain or loss for U.S. federal tax purposes.

Q-3: Must a taxpayer who receives virtual currency as payment for goods or services include in computing gross income the fair market value of the virtual currency?

A-3: Yes. A taxpayer who receives virtual currency as payment for goods or services must, in computing gross income, include the fair market value of the virtual currency, measured in U.S. dollars, as of the date that the virtual currency was received. See Publication 525, Taxable and Nontaxable Income, for more information on miscellaneous income from exchanges involving property or services.

Q-4: What is the basis of virtual currency received as payment for goods or services in Q&A-3?

A-4: The basis of virtual currency that a taxpayer receives as payment for goods or services in Q&A-3 is the fair market value of the virtual currency in U.S. dollars as of the date of receipt. See Publication 551, Basis of Assets, for more information on the computation of basis when property is received for goods or services.

Q-5: How is the fair market value of virtual currency determined?

A-5: For U.S. tax purposes, transactions using virtual currency must be reported in U.S. dollars. Therefore, taxpayers will be required to determine the fair market value of virtual currency in U.S. dollars as of the date of payment or receipt. If a virtual currency is listed on an exchange and the exchange rate is established by market supply and demand, the fair market value of the virtual currency is determined by converting the virtual currency into U.S.

dollars (or into another real currency which in turn can be converted into U.S. dollars) at the exchange rate, in a reasonable manner that is consistently applied.

Q-6: Does a taxpayer have gain or loss upon an exchange of virtual currency for other property?

A-6: Yes. If the fair market value of property received in exchange for virtual currency exceeds the taxpayer's adjusted basis of the virtual currency, the taxpayer has taxable gain. The taxpayer has a loss if the fair market value of the property received is less than the adjusted basis of the virtual currency. See Publication 544, Sales and Other Dispositions of Assets, for information about the tax treatment of sales and exchanges, such as whether a loss is deductible.

Q-7: What type of gain or loss does a taxpayer realize on the sale or exchange of virtual currency?

A-7: The character of the gain or loss generally depends on whether the virtual currency is a capital asset in the hands of the taxpayer. A taxpayer generally realizes capital gain or loss on the sale or exchange of virtual currency that is a capital asset in the hands of the taxpayer. For example, stocks, bonds, and other investment property are generally capital assets. A taxpayer generally realizes ordinary gain or loss on the sale or exchange of virtual currency that is not a capital asset in the hands of the taxpayer. Inventory and other property held mainly for sale to customers in a trade or business are examples of property that is not a capital asset. See Publication 544 for more information about capital assets and the character of gain or loss.

Q-8: Does a taxpayer who "mines" virtual currency (for example, uses computer resources to validate Bitcoin transactions and maintain the public Bitcoin transaction ledger) realize gross income upon receipt of the virtual currency resulting from those activities?

A-8: Yes, when a taxpayer successfully "mines" virtual currency, the fair market value of the virtual currency as of the date of receipt is includible in gross income. See Publication 525, Taxable and Nontaxable Income, for more information on taxable income.

Q-9: Is an individual who "mines" virtual currency as a trade or business subject to self-employment tax on the income derived from those activities?

A-9: If a taxpayer's "mining" of virtual currency constitutes a trade or business, and the "mining" activity is not undertaken by the taxpayer as an employee, the net earnings from self-employment (generally, gross income derived from carrying on a trade or business less allowable deductions) resulting from those activities constitute self-employment income and are subject to the self-employment tax. See Chapter 10 of Publication 334, *Tax Guide for Small Business*, for more information on self-employment tax and Publication 535, *Business Expenses*, for more information on determining whether expenses are from a business activity carried on to make a profit.

Q-10: Does virtual currency received by an independent contractor for performing services constitute self-employment income?

A-10: Yes. Generally, self-employment income includes all gross income derived by an individual from any trade or business carried on by the individual as other than an employee. Consequently, the fair market value of virtual currency received for services performed as an independent contractor, measured in U.S. dollars as of the date of receipt, constitutes self-employment income and is subject to the self-employment tax. See FS-2007-18, April 2007, *Business or Hobby? Answer Has Implications for Deductions*, for information on determining whether an activity is a business or a hobby.

Q-11: Does virtual currency paid by an employer as remuneration for services constitute wages for employment tax purposes?

A-11: Yes. Generally, the medium in which remuneration for services is paid is immaterial to the determination of whether the remuneration constitutes wages for employment tax purposes. Consequently, the fair market value of virtual currency paid as wages is subject to federal income tax withholding, Federal Insurance Contributions Act (FICA) tax, and Federal Unemployment Tax Act (FUTA) tax and must be reported on Form W-2, *Wage and Tax Statement*. See Publication 15 (Circular E), *Employer's Tax Guide*, for information on the withholding, depositing, reporting, and paying of employment taxes.

Q-12: Is a payment made using virtual currency subject to information reporting?

A-12: A payment made using virtual currency is subject to information reporting to the same extent as any other payment made in property. For example, a person who in the course of a trade or business makes a payment of fixed and determinable income using virtual currency with a value of $600 or more to a U.S. non-exempt recipient in a taxable year is required to report the payment to the IRS and to the payee. Examples of payments of fixed and determinable income include rent, salaries, wages, premiums, annuities, and compensation.

Q-13: Is a person who in the course of a trade or business makes a payment using virtual currency worth $600 or more to an independent contractor for performing services required to file an information return with the IRS?

A-13: Generally, a person who in the course of a trade or business makes a payment of $600 or more in a taxable year to an independent contractor for the performance of services is required to report that payment to the IRS and to the payee on Form 1099- MISC, *Miscellaneous Income*. Payments of virtual currency required to be reported on Form 1099-MISC should be reported using the fair market value of the virtual currency in U.S. dollars as of the date of payment. The payment recipient may have income even if the recipient does not receive a Form 1099-MISC. See the Instructions to Form 1099-MISC and the General Instructions for Certain Information Returns for more information. For payments to non-U.S. persons, see Publication 515, *Withholding of Tax on Nonresident Aliens and Foreign Entities.*

Q-14: Are payments made using virtual currency subject to backup withholding?

A-14: Payments made using virtual currency are subject to backup withholding to the same extent as other payments made in property. Therefore, payors making reportable payments using virtual currency must solicit a taxpayer identification number (TIN) from the payee. The payor must backup withhold from the payment if a TIN is not obtained prior to payment or if the payor receives notification from the IRS that backup withholding is required. See Publication 1281, *Backup Withholding for Missing and Incorrect Name/TINs,* for more information.

Q-15: Are there IRS information reporting requirements for a person who settles payments made in virtual currency on behalf of merchants that accept virtual currency from their customers?

A-15: Yes, if certain requirements are met. In general, a third party that contracts with a substantial number of unrelated merchants to settle payments between the merchants and their customers is a third-party settlement organization (TPSO). A TPSO is required to report payments made to a merchant on a Form 1099-K, *Payment Card and Third Party Network Transactions*, if, for the calendar year, both (1) the number of transactions settled for the merchant exceeds 200, and (2) the gross amount of payments made to the merchant exceeds $20,000. When completing Boxes 1, 3, and 5a-1 on the Form 1099-K, transactions where the TPSO settles payments made with virtual currency are aggregated with transactions where the TPSO settles payments made with real currency to determine the total amounts to be reported in those boxes. When determining whether the transactions are reportable, the value of the virtual currency is the fair market value of the virtual currency in U.S. dollars on the date of payment. See The Third Party Information Reporting Center, http://www.irs.gov/TaxProfessionals/Third-Party-Reporting-Information-Center, for more information on reporting transactions on Form 1099-K.

Q-16: Will taxpayers be subject to penalties for having treated a virtual currency transaction in a manner that is inconsistent with this notice prior to March 25, 2014?

A-16: Taxpayers may be subject to penalties for failure to comply with tax laws. For example, underpayments attributable to virtual currency transactions may be subject to penalties, such as accuracy-related penalties under §6662. In addition, failure to timely or correctly report virtual currency transactions when required to do so may be subject to information reporting penalties under §6721 and §6722. However, penalty relief may be available to taxpayers and persons required to file an information return who are able to establish that the underpayment or failure to properly file information returns is due to reasonable cause.

Section 5. Drafting Information

The principal author of this notice is Keith A. Aqui of the Office of Associate Chief Counsel (Income Tax & Accounting). For further information about income tax issues addressed in this notice, please contact Mr. Aqui at (202) 317-4718; for further information about employment tax issues addressed in this notice, please contact Mr. Neil D. Shepherd at (202) 317- 4774; for further information about information reporting issues addressed in this notice, please contact Ms. Adrienne E. Griffin at (202) 317- 6845; and for further information regarding foreign currency issues addressed in this notice, please contact Mr. Raymond J. Stahl at (202) 317- 6938. These are not toll-free calls.

Appendix 2:
Excel Calculations for a Series of Purchases And Sales

THIS APPENDIX IS DEVOTED TO a step-by-step series of spreadsheet calculations showing the determination of gains.

Let's say we started in virtual currency by cleverly dollar-cost-averaging our way in at a rate of $100 per month. The spreadsheet on the next page shows how we'd record these purchases.

Date Purch	# BTC Purch	Unit Value	Purch Price	Fees	Cost Basis
1/1/2015	0.31855	$313.92	$100.00	$1.49	$101.49
2/1/2015	0.44170	$226.40	$100.00	$1.49	$101.49
3/1/2015	0.38649	$258.74	$100.00	$1.49	$101.49
4/1/2015	0.40560	$246.55	$100.00	$1.49	$101.49
5/1/2015	0.43081	$232.12	$100.00	$1.49	$101.49
6/1/2015	0.44781	$223.31	$100.00	$1.49	$101.49
7/1/2015	0.38811	$257.66	$100.00	$1.49	$101.49
8/1/2015	0.35709	$280.04	$100.00	$1.49	$101.49
9/1/2015	0.43985	$227.35	$100.00	$1.49	$101.49

Date Purch	# BTC Purch	Unit Value	Purch Price	Fees	Cost Basis
10/1/2015	0.42093	$237.57	$100.00	$1.49	$101.49
11/1/2015	0.30762	$325.08	$100.00	$1.49	$101.49
12/1/2015	0.27569	$362.73	$100.00	$1.49	$101.49

Since there were no sales in 2015, we have nothing to report on our tax return.

In 2016, we decide to cleverly dollar-cost-average our way out. We have a total of 4.62025 BTC; we want to sell all of it in 2016 but, mindful of our holding period, we decide to start in February. Dividing 4.62025 by eleven months means that we should sell 0.42002 BTC from February to November, then sell off the remaining 0.42005 BTC in December. Here's what the sales look like.

Date Sold	# BTC Sold	Unit Value	Proceeds	Fee
2/1/2016	0.42002	$371.25	$155.93	$2.32
3/1/2016	0.42002	$433.64	$182.14	$2.71
4/1/2016	0.42002	$417.01	$175.15	$2.61
5/1/2016	0.42002	$453.04	$190.29	$2.84
6/1/2016	0.42002	$536.42	$225.31	$3.36
7/1/2016	0.42002	$676.52	$284.15	$4.23
8/1/2016	0.42002	$607.37	$255.11	$3.80
9/1/2016	0.42002	$571.69	$240.12	$3.58
10/1/2016	0.42002	$613.93	$257.86	$3.84
11/1/2016	0.42002	$729.27	$306.31	$4.56
12/1/2016	0.42005	$753.25	$316.40	$4.71

Now we'll step through the tax implications of the sales, one sale at a time, using the FIFO method. We'll start with the February sale. Because we only purchased 0.31855 BTC in January of 2015, we'll have to sell some of our February 2015 BTC as well. It looks like this:

	Date Sold	# BTC Sold	Unit Value	Proceeds	Fee	Total
Sold	2/1/2016	0.42002	$371.25	$155.93	$2.32	$158.26
Purch	1/1/2015	0.31855	$313.92	$(100.00)	$(1.49)	$(101.49)
Purch	2/1/2015	0.10147	$226.40	$(22.97)	$(0.34)	$(23.31)

Note that fees are recorded at a percentage of 1.49%.

Because we didn't pay quite *enough* attention to our holding period, the BTC purchased on February 1st of 2015 and sold on February 1st of 2016 will be short-term gain, not long term. So we have to add an extra step and divide the sale into two pieces: 0.031855 and 0.10147 BTC.

Feb. Sale	Date Sold	# BTC Sold	Unit Value	Proceeds	Fee	Total
Sold	2/1/2016	0.31855	$371.25	$118.26	$1.76	$120.02
Purchased	1/1/2015	0.31855	$313.92	$(100.00)	$(1.49)	$(101.49)
Long Term Gain						**$18.53**
Sold	2/1/2016	0.10147	$371.25	$37.67	$(0.56)	$37.11
Purchased	2/1/2015	0.10147	$226.40	$(22.97)	$(0.34)	$(23.31)
Short Term Gain						**$13.80**

March, April and May sales:

Mar. Sale	Date Sold	# BTC Sold	Unit Value	Proceeds	Fee	Total
Sold	3/1/2016	0.34023	$433.64	$147.54	$2.20	$149.74
Purchased	2/1/2015	0.34023	$226.40	$(77.03)	$(1.15)	$(78.18)
Long Term Gain						**$71.56**
Sold	3/1/2016	0.07979	$433.64	$34.60	$0.52	$35.12
Purchased	3/1/2015	0.07979	$258.74	$(20.64)	$(0.31)	$(20.95)
Short Term Gain						**$14.17**

Apr. Sale	Date Sold	# BTC Sold	Unit Value	Proceeds	Fee	Total
Sold	4/1/2016	0.30670	$417.01	$127.90	$1.91	$129.80
Purchased	3/1/2015	0.30670	$258.74	$(79.36)	$(1.54)	$(80.90)
Long Term Gain						**$48.90**
Sold	4/1/2016	0.11332	$417.01	$47.26	$0.71	$47.97
Purchased	4/1/2015	0.11332	$246.55	$(27.97)	$(0.42)	$(28.36)
Short Term Gain						**$19.61**

May Sale	Date Sold	# BTC Sold	Unit Value	Proceeds	Fee	Total
Sold	5/1/2016	0.29228	$453.04	$132.41	$1.97	$134.39
Purchased	4/1/2015	0.29228	$246.55	$(72.06)	$(1.07)	$(73.13)
Long Term Gain						**$61.26**
Sold	5/1/2016	0.12774	$453.04	$57.87	$0.86	$58.73
Purchased	5/1/2015	0.12774	$232.12	$(29.65)	$(0.44)	$(30.09)
Short Term Gain						**$28.64**

And, hopefully, you now see how it works.

CPSIA information can be obtained
at www.ICGtesting.com
Printed in the USA
LVHW02s0448261217
560802LV00019B/486/P